The secret formula

The 10 best guides to succeed in affiliate marketing

Table of contents

Presentation

Affiliate marketing is a publicizing model in which an organization remunerates outsider distributors to create traffic or prompts the organization's items and administrations. The outsider distributors are subsidiaries, and the commission expense boosts them to track down ways of advancing the organization.

Assuming that you are simply beginning or have been doing member promoting for quite a while, following these ten stages will assist with working on your odds of coming out on top.

Each tip gives an understanding of the strategies involved by the best advertisers in the business.

Partner Marketing Tips

Make strong substance

Track your prosperity

Know your items

Connect with your guests

Focus on one specialty

Give data and help, as opposed to sell

Pick the right items

Continuously be trying and getting to
the next level

Commit the time
Set legitimate assumptions

Chapter 1

Make strong substance

If you hope to make additional payments from member advertising, you should make the quality substance. Content is in each piece of correspondence you use. You will require information on suggestions to take action both enlightening, as well as value-based, and the capacity to write in an extensively coherent manner.

You additionally need to make your substance peruser driven. Answer their inquiries, and give them definite data, however, written in a way that is open and locked in.

Understand what your listeners might be thinking, and see what carries them to your site. A hunt box is a phenomenal method for realizing what they need to track down on your site.

Compose, compose, compose. Focus on making ordinary substances.

Content showcasing can be a decent decision for subsidiaries for various reasons:

Fabricates Trust: Trust is one of the mystery ingredients for transformation. Individuals perusing an item survey might be bound to buy the items or administrations you suggest if they know what your identity is and they trust your perspective.

Assembles Awareness: It gets you before individuals and constructs mindfulness.

Increments Organic Traffic: A quality substance that positions well on Google can drive more individuals to your site/greeting page and so on.

Expands Targeted Traffic: A very much planned content promoting methodology can carry individuals to you that are bound to make a buy in your specialty.

Web-based Entertainment Friendly: Good happiness might be shared on social expanding mindfulness and traffic further.

Develops Your Email List: If email showcasing is essential for your methodology you can utilize content to build supporters of your rundown, giving you one more channel to advertise with.

Can Help with SEO for Your Website: Posting normal, the great-quality substance could assist with expanding your site's perceivability on Google look.

Chapter 2

Track your associate promoting achievement

Progressing achievement needs bits of knowledge concerning what has worked previously. While you would rather not set it and fail to remember it - knowing how guests draw in with your site is significant. Search positioning will have an effect, as will social sharing, and so forth.

You want to utilize your guest examination to find out about your guests. Which rates are new as opposed to bringing visitors back? What pages get most of your traffic? What joins in your route bar and different puts on each page get clicked? This multitude of inquiries will give responses that you can use to improve and add activities.

Where is your changing over traffic coming from? What pages are visited most before a transformation? Utilize your examination to find solutions you can use to figure out what new satisfaction is required or even where to put specific connections on existing pages. Utilize your information!

To put it, by following measurements, you're observing the outcome of your advertising endeavors. This will assist you with developing your business. Without measurements, you can't understand what you're doing well or off-base as a member. As a member program supervisor, you can't realize which subsidiaries have the most transformations in your network.

Chapter 3

Know your items

Information can recognize you from your rivals. As a subsidiary you are making proposals to your guests on different items, so to stand apart you should be viewed as a specialist, or if nothing else a spot to get nitty gritty data about the items you advance.

Over and over again members get a couple of merchants they think will hold any importance with their guests without getting to know them. Regardless of whether you are not giving surveys of these items, you need to know how they work and what benefits they can give clients. Try not to join with another merchant since they seem to offer something in your specialty - properly investigate things. Take a gander at the surveys others have done to begin, however, attempt and use it yourself, regardless of whether it is only the demo.

Item information is a fundamental deal ability. Understanding your items' elements permits you to introduce their advantages precisely and influentially. Clients answer energetic deals staff who are enthusiastic about their items and anxious to impart the advantages to them.

Chapter 4

Draw in your guests

Best subsidiary advertisers converse with their guests. If you have a blog, permit remarks. This will furnish you with the chance to discuss with your guests. Indeed, you should sift through the spam, yet assuming that you answer to the vast majority of your analysts and begin discoursed, they will get back to proceed with the discussion.

Pose inquiries toward the finish of a blog entry. "What different elements ought to be incorporated?" "Would you like more data on this theme?" "Let us know your perspective!" These invitations to take action will assist with cultivating local area connections. While answering, utilize the analysts' names at every possible opportunity.

The more your guests come to see your site as a local area of similar individuals, the more they will return and expand your changes.

In the consistently cutthroat travel and the travel industry area, and presently like never before previously, organizations need to supercharge promoting endeavors to drive traffic and accomplish an upper hand. One technique I've observed that produces dependable outcomes is member showcasing. A hearty travel member network draws in a powerful group of powerhouses who will showcase your image (with payments procured from advancing an organization or potentially driving a deal) while offering you the chance to take advantage of their crowd. A commonly gainful organization's likewise practical: you just compensate for results.

At the point when you join forces with powerhouses who have an enormous following or a critical arrival in your industry, they can essentially raise brand mindfulness, increment traffic to your site, and lead to explicit outcomes: more deals. Similarly as significantly, when your partner puts your movement image before their crowd, your arrival at increases and you can become your base of new clients huge amounts at a time. Furthermore, because you possibly pay when a deal goes through, partner showcasing can convey a dependable profit from speculation. Here are a few demonstrated approaches to utilizing it to make a devoted following.

Pick the right partners
Member showcasing permits you to use the force of impact to get individuals to purchase from you, yet for that to work you'll have to have the right subsidiaries. A decent one for your movement image ought to have:

• Incredible compatibility with their crowd.

• A group of people that is keen on your image/administration.

Chapter 5

Focus on one specialty associate business

Time and again offshoot advertisers utilize a shotgun approach, getting whatever the number of items could reasonably be expected to push when they ought to zero in on their principal interest and specialty-related items. If you have any desire to foster a fruitful partner showcasing site, consistently stick to one specialty. You can make different locales to advance different specialties, yet don't extend yourself excessively far, because that will prompt flimsy substance destinations.

Center around a market specialty is significant because even a specialist member advertiser can't offer everything to everyone. For individuals to get impacted by an advertiser, the advertiser initially needs to set up a good foundation for himself/herself as a well-informed authority. A specialist by definition knows a ton about a little subject. Consequently, partner showcasing, by definition is the round of specialties! Any associate advertiser focusing on the whole web, moving from items to items taking a stab at whatever gives the greatest commission will figure out that they aren't exactly ready to sell anything. Member showcasing is tied in with utilizing specialties to limit your concentration and afterward expanding your endeavors once the degree has been recognized.

Strategically pitching Benefits in a Marketing Niche

A few advantages emerge out of zeroing in on a market specialty. Strategically pitching is one of these advantages. Purchasers would rather not buy inconsequential items on the counsel given by an associate advertiser. Nonetheless, assuming they are purchasing related items, they wouldn't fret about spending the extra dollars assuming that they accept that the guidance being given is authentic and impartial. Laying down a good foundation for yourself as a specialist permits you to strategically pitch a few items to a buyer and procure a commission on every one of them. Be that as it may, notoriety is key here! Purchasers should accept that you are just contributing whatever is best for them. Assuming they accept that the member has ulterior intentions, the believability is lost and this misfortune makes an incredibly unfriendly difference.

Economies of Scale and Market Niche
Subsidiary advertisers can likewise exploit economies of scale when they confine their exercises to a promoting specialty. This is because when they become a specialist in the specialty, they can haggle more ideal arrangements with merchants selling related items. As referenced above, strategically pitching of related items is generally simple

when mastery and authority have been laid out.

Likewise, the gradual exertion expected to advance an extra item isn't exceptionally high. A similar blog entry can be utilized to advance a few articles by including a couple of lines. Any income created is steady since the endeavors required are not extremely high.

Choosing the Right Niche
Choosing the right specialty is a significant ability for an associate advertiser. There are a few rules that can be observed to get improved results. They are :

Pick a specialty where you have a mastery of some kind. Instructive as well as expert skill isn't needed for progress in the offshoot showcasing the game. Nonetheless, they in all actuality do make life impressively simple as partners need to strive to acquire trust! Try not to pick a specialty that is a trend or the "in thing" at some random 16 ounces of time. It draws in a ton of fleeting partners. These offshoots make the commissions drop till they are as of now not reasonable and afterward leave the market. Likewise, the sellers in these business sectors may not be areas of strength monetarily. Consider stable specialties that have been there for quite a long time and will show up into the indefinite future!

The size of the specialty ought not to be excessively little. More modest specialties are not difficult to catch. Be that as it may, they are sufficiently not to acquire fair commissions. For the business to be reasonable, it must be adaptable somewhat.

Subsequently, for an offshoot advertiser, it is fundamental to find a market specialty and spotlight the endeavors on that specialty as opposed to the market overall. The thought is to be a hotshot in a little lake as opposed to losing all sense of direction in the huge sea that the web has become!

Chapter 6

Give data and help, as opposed to sell

Conspicuous deals and self-advancement locales never get forward momentum. You want to help your guests and give quality data they find valuable with the goal that they make want more. Assuming you take a gander at the locales that rank well for the different terms utilized in your specialty, you will find that helpful data wins out. Investigate as needs are and give more subtleties or refreshed data.

Data and assist with furnishing your offshoot program with a genuinely necessary lift to assist it with remaining serious and successful. By searching it out, you get important data like patterns, strategies, and general counsel you can use to fortify your image.

Here, we covered three distinct ways you can develop your industry information:

Organization to foster proficient connections.
Tap into industry news for modern data.
Go to gatherings to get close enough to master experiences.

Chapter 7

Pick the right items

Picking a decent item is a vital element for getting deals, and to ensure that you have picked a decent item, you can, through a straightforward hunt on the Google web crawler, realize all the item subtleties and client sentiments.

To track down the right item or administration to advance on offshoot showcasing, you want to initially find a specialty that you are most inspired by and that you have more information about. Then, at that point, find items or administrations connected with that specialty and advance.

Pick an item with which you are natural since certain clients pose inquiries in regards to the item while you furnish them with a partner connect, so you should have a decent grasp on the item or administration you are selling.

Likewise, do some exploration and apply for the high commission program that will assist you with procuring more in a short measure of time.

Chapter 8

Continuously be trying and getting to the next level

You ought to continuously be attempting to work on your interaction. Test length, utilization of diagram, different workmanship, and different elements. Member advertising, similar to any educational experience, is a continuous exertion. While large numbers of the means above can be executed toward the beginning, you need to learn and improve as you go.

Advancing your offshoot showcasing system will assist with creating leads and further developing transformation rates. The best way to get an unmistakable image of which of your showcasing thoughts and parts function admirably is to test them against each other. Testing various methodologies is likewise an incredible method for utilizing transient margin time, as it can prompt expanded transformations when things get back once more.

One of the most useful puts to zero in on while advancing is the presentation of points of arrival with extraordinary showcasing points associated with your mission. Here is an outline of how to specialty and test different greeting pages for the best outcomes.

Life systems of a Landing Page
A quality greeting page is a deciding component in any member program's

prosperity.Three(3)_fundamental substance parts make uplanders, and they should be streamlined to attract guests and convince them to make a move.

Title - The title is expected to grab the peruser's eye. It ought to make page guests need to keep perusing by engaging their responsibility and introducing your center thought obviously and briefly.

Duplicate -The duplicate is the principal collection of text on a greeting page. It should be sufficiently convincing to keep the guest perusing and written in a manner that imparts your message. Perusers ought to rapidly get a handle on the thing you are offering and why it will help them.

Source of inspiration (CTA) - Once the peruser understands what you are offering and is persuaded that it is appropriate for them, the source of inspiration tells them what to do straight away. It might request that they get in touch with you, make a buy, download a record, or pursue a record, contingent upon the item or administration you offer.

Making Different Marketing Angles

The composed substance on a greeting page ought to be made to recount a particular story. This is otherwise called the promoting point. Settling on a point will assist with centering your title, duplicate, and source of inspiration. Your point, thusly, will be educated by what it is that you are offering and who you are offering it to. The objective is to interface sincerely with your main interest group and cause them to feel a specific way about the proposition in a way that will in a perfect world lead to transformations.

To concoct a useful point, you should pick and research an objective segment. Consider who it is that you are promoting in light of variables like orientation and age. Your substance might look altogether different relying upon the crowd you are attempting to speak to. Attempt to place yourself in the shoes of your objective segment and contemplate what latest things or world occasions could permit you to all the more likely associate with them.

Conceptualizing different showcasing points offers you the chance to foster innovative procedures that assist you with standing apart from contenders. Featuring your extraordinary specialty is consistently a valuable promoting approach, and it is especially significant on the off chance that you are in an oversaturated market.

Step-by-step instructions to Test Your Marketing Strategies
Whenever you have settled on a few distinct points and made content given those points, the time has come to figure out which ones perform best. You can try out showcasing procedures with what is known as a split test or A/B test. A split test is essentially contrasting two distinct variants (rendition An and form

B) of a presentation page to see which one prompts more changes. Playing out a split test makes it simple to evaluate two showcasing points and conclude which one is a superior fit for your proposition.

The primary advances engaged with playing out the A/B test are:

Part your approaching traffic equitably between two distinct variants of a greeting page that you wish to test.

1. Keep running the two pages until you have accumulated an adequate number of information to make significant determinations.

2. Cautiously report your outcomes and use them to frame speculation about whether any extra changes might prompt more transformations.

3. Run extra tests, if vital, to additionally enhance the greeting page.

Testing different showcasing points utilizing a split test will tell you what sorts of content your interest group answers. With this information, you will want to make profoundly custom-fitted missions that convey results.

Quality Content for Effective Landing Page Testing
To run split tests that give you valuable data, you will require quality greeting pages that focus on your different

advertising points. This is where Constant Content can help. Our group of experienced authors will make all of the greeting pages you expect for any testing technique. We will furnish you with exceptional and significant substance for your designated crowds. Then, you should simply send off the mission and see which procedures acquire the transformations you are searching for.

Chapter 9

Commit the time

To become effective you want to put the time in. Partner showcasing requires continuous exertion, so be ready and assign ordinary time for your endeavors.

In the underlying days of your Affiliate Marketing, I would agree that base committed 4 hours required assuming that you are thinking about procuring as automated revenue. To consider it as a fundamental kind of revenue, I would agree that work on no less than 8 hours daily committed to comprehending and gaining proficiency with a few parts of the business.

Spend around 2 to 3 hours out of each day on your member business

That is more than enough to get you to $5000 to $10.000 each month
You don't have to invest a lot of energy

You simply have to ensure you center your restricted investment on the right assignments, exercises, and activities

We as a whole got 24 hours out of every day
Is about how we spend and what we do in that 24 hours

Isn't ABOUT BEING BUSY IS ABOUT BEING PRODUCTIVE

So not all assignments are made equivalent. Some value all the more than others

Here are some model

- Low compensation exercises

- building website and specialized know-how
- conversing with inadequate possibilities
- investing energy in youtube watching one video after other
- going on your telephone
- noting messages
- Illustration of lucrative exercises

- Driving designated traffic to your offers

- Statistical surveying
- copywriting making an items Conversing with qualified possibilities

There was an illustration of high or significant activities

A lot of subsidiary marketers and business visionaries
Invest energy on things that don't push their business ahead

Asking why they can't make money
As I said is no point simply being occupied you became useful
You could deal with your business for 10 hours every day except doing every one of some unacceptable things
Then again you can chip away at your business 2 hours of the day

What's more, you could get by from it

Every time you are going to do anything
for your business
Ask yourself if is this significant or not.

Assuming isn't significant don't make it
happen, do the significant assignment
first
Then, at that point, do different things
So you don't require a lot of time
You simply have to utilize the time you
have well overall

Most business people go the entire day
sitting idle
What's more, they could do 2 hours of
useful work a day and waste the wide
range of various hours

I trust this made a difference
Assuming you want more assistance in
partner showcasing
Is across the board stages
Giving you all that you want to prevail
with member marketing

Chapter 10

Set legitimate assumptions

You won't make 1,000,000 bucks in a month. You want to set practical assumptions. Many partners invest a limited measure of energy to work out their unique locales and then focus on a more modest sum to continue adding content while beginning another site. Whether you have a solitary site with a concentrated continuous turn of events or various at first more modest destinations, put forth objectives and work towards achieving them.

Get significant guidance for your subsidiary advertising site that can drive traffic.

Figure out how to make item surveys that assist online purchasers with concluding whether they will purchase something.

(I) Choosing the Right Domain for your associate promoting business.

(ii) Choosing the Right Hosting For Affiliate Marketing
Figure out how speed and dependability can help your partner site perform better in search and then some.
Involving SSL Certificates in Affiliate Marketing

That little lock image is a big deal to your perusers. Realize which ones are ideal for your site

The most effective method to make a fruitful member showcasing site

Get noteworthy counsel on making an offshoot promoting site that drives traffic and deals.

Step-by-step instructions to compose convincing surveys.

Figure out how you can turn into a confided-in hotspot for item data while developing another inflow of money.

(iii) Picking A Niche In Affiliate Marketing

Figure out how to offset your advantages with different elements to find the best specialty for your member advertising site.

(iv) Using Analytics Data to Improve Affiliate Sales

Understanding examination and information investigation assist effective subsidiaries with keeping cutthroat deals.